Watching Her Walk

by

Craig Murray

This publication is a creative work protected in full by all applicable copyright laws, as well as by misappropriation, trade secret, unfair competition, and other applicable laws. No part of this book may be reproduced or transmitted in any manner without written permission from Netherwood Books, except in the case of brief quotations embodied in critical articles or reviews. All rights reserved.

Watching Her Walk

COPYRIGHT © 2011 by Craig Murray
First Ebook Edition, July 2011, Willow Moon Publishing
Second Ebook/Print Edition, July 2013
ISBN 978-0-9878570-4-0

Photograph by Craig Murray

Dedication

There are always so many people to thank and to acknowledge whenever a work is written. No writer writes alone, it is the interactions, the loves, the helps, all the people who have in their own way contributed to the story. But decisions have to be made both for brevity and function so please, if you are not named, at least know you are remembered.

To Margaret and Fiona without whose patience and love this would not have been possible.

To My grandparents, Major John McAdam HLI MBE and Mary Corrigan McAdam whose never ending support of my writing helped in so many ways

To Ailsa and Susan for so much help over so many years, To Anna for all her help and to Kate, you will always be missed.

Shades of Sand

What was I before I ask the void, the shades of sand,
The cracked amphora that held the royal crimson of lost days.
I had no limbs, a tree bereft was I,
Joshua at the edge of forever,
Skin pressed tight into dried rivers of bark.
I was blind to all the hues that painted memory,
That coloured the cheeks of childhood
and smelled of early summer grass,
Verdant soft.
Almost deaf, ears heard rumbles and groans,
the discordancy of one,
The symphonic cacophony of shattered glass and sliding tears,
This I was before.
Before what asked my heart, its voice supple, gentle.
Before what asked my soul, Childlike, waiting in wonder.
Before I say, listen to my words, before, before.
For now I hear the laughter of stars and see
the dancing of the waves,
Now my arms embrace love and feel a gentleness eternal
And I soar with symphonies as yet undreamt of,
But that is now I say.
What was I before, I was less, I was little, before I loved.

Collecting Stars

I shall collect the stars
Wind strewn and scattered
In the coils of her hair

I will gather unto me
The brilliant faceted diamonds
That twinkle in her eyes

I shall wrap up and hold
The deepest silver sheen
Of her summer dampened skin

And even with these things
I could still not weave a tapestry
To match the beauty of her soul

Islands

Mocha dusted porcelain
And almond eyes
A tiny doll
A question of geisha

The unintentional grace
Of supple limbs
And delicate movements
Of tiny flowers

She speaks of
Silk roads and spiders webs
Deep green seas
And far away mountains

Islands peek above
Misty waves
A fathomless blue
To tempt the swimmer

And So

And so I love, and there amongst
These blooms I know will fade
Contentment flowers majestically.
Am I such a fool to gather these
Tiny buds, whisper to them secrets
And tell them of their immortality
Better I gazed with jaundiced eye
Secure in knowing grey follows dawn
And all things fall like autumn leaves
But to love wildly majestically to know
And to ignore the knowledge happily
Loving first worrying second hoping most

Knowing

I always knew and I've always lied.
Deception the blanket a lover hides behind.
It was always in your eyes,
The slight curl of your smile.
The way you protested when asked.
The way you hesitated when caught.
The way you were.
The way you are.
The way you always will be.
And what I lost when at last that door closed.
When I boarded the plane and left forever.
I lost her smiles and laughter.
Soft skin and willing easy flesh.
I lost dreams and promises, hopes and more than all.

I lost the chance for her to lie when it might really matter.

I Lost Her One Day

I lost her one day and then
Did not know it for months
Packed and gone without a note
Not even the simplest goodbye
She hated me then although
She says she hated herself more
We were a fantasy of smoke
Of worn sweaters and that shack
We would have hidden within
Wrote poetry, ate meagerly
Bohemia relocated to the foot
Of distant brown mountains
I lost her one day and then
When found she simply said
Sorry, she no longer lives here

Spinning

Spinning in place
And laughing at leaves
The wind catches her hair
And it dances
To a beat of its own

Exhausted and panting
She falls to the grass
To lie still and silent
Amongst the flowers
And dreams of eternity

Angel

Angelic smiles
And fearsome growls
Manic behaviour and
Tickling laughter
A treasure chest of love
Resides in her heart
A running conundrum
Of little girl pleasures
She leaves us laughing
And aching with joy
Gathering flowers
And rocks for throwing
She is our sun
And reason for smiling

A first Meeting

And in that first meeting,
That time of magic and wonder.
When souls refreshed, reborn were given
First hint of all that might be, could be.
And when we kissed
And the world became
A small and personal thing,
When nothing was left but us,
There lay eternity.
And then when night slipped into day,
When our moment passed and now
Were forced to leave.
Return to the commonplace of our lives,
We swore. Loyalty and fealty, loves eternal grasp.
We would not lose this treasure found.
I should have known that in your oaths
Lay the pregnancy of its death.

Far from Forges

Where once there beat such a pulse
As hot as mighty Vulcan's forge
Where hammers struck the anvils
Of my heart with blows resounding
Now there is a flat and empty space
Where memory is distant gray
Sorrow or loss another's concern
As truth and immateriality replace
She is a ghost thing in her hollows
A fable once told but no longer believed
And I gaze upon the flat and see
there was little enough to begin with
I wonder when like ancient sheets
She dimmed and frayed stained yellow
No day or word stands out required
To verify her passing from is to not
Now knowing that she can only be
All she was and is and will be forever
How strange these mad tables turn
Where I might grow while she decays

Mimi Dies

O soave fanciulla, how I wept for you at meeting
knowing that even then the shades of death linger.

O dolce viso, perfect countenance, dying eyes,
I sought a truth and found consumptions hunger

Ah, tu sol comandi, amor, just not this heart
not this place, love rules but here, loss approaches

No, per pieta, arguments unheeded, warnings lost
you seek comforts in sheets soaked with horror

Amore, amore, amore, I felt your fingers in mine
our hands intertwined and the tears in my eyes,

I knew, I always knew. Mimi was always dying

*

O soave fanciulla ~ Oh Lovely Girl
O Dolce viso ~ Oh Beautiful Face
Ah, tu sol comandi, amor ~ Ah, you rule alone, love
No, per pieta ~ No pity for
Amore ~ love

Limber Lithe

And could you love me, limber lithe,
Could you rest your hand upon my shoulder,
Feel the scars beneath this sleeve
And still find faith within my eyes?

And could you love me limber lithe,
Could you place your head upon my chest,
Feel my heart and all its wounds
And still find hope within its depths?

And could you love me limber lithe,
Could you take me to your bed,
Chase away my savage ghosts,
And love me for all I am?

And could you love me limber lithe?

Run Away

Run away with me
To where the grass is soft
Azure skies beckon and the sun is painted
With golden brush-strokes
A thousand spices fill the air
As the creak of ships at anchor
Speak of impossible seas
Run away with me
Leave behind your fear
And poverty
Your traumas and deceits
And accept mine

I Will Sleep

All the why's are said,

All that remains are the whispers of solace.

Drip the blood from your stigmata

Into my eyes,

Blind me and bind me and lose your fears.

I grow stronger in my defence,

My resolve,

But I still need somewhere

Safe to sleep

There is perfection in slumbering knowledge,

In quiet, in laying down my shield, my greaves,

In finding she, in finding where,

The noises are quieted and that,

Just that, is all that is needed.

Wrap me in your skirts,

Enfold me in your arms,

I will sleep

Sotto Voce

Sotto voce
As I add you to my gathered tragedies
Summer blooms are grey and the forest
Filled with the wandering dead pleading
She spoke in hollow mimicry better silence
Than listen to the mournful strings cutting
Truth and flowers stuffed toys my heart
Sotto voce

Aurora

Leaping from star to star he hangs his hat on the moon
And laughs at the simple pleasure.
Aurora, will you sing to me of ancient men
Who held the world upon their shoulders,
Who drank the draught of the ocean,
Who yielded to none but infamies flaming sword.
No she says,
These tales are not yours but ages long since dust
upon the ledge.
Carve out your own tales in the hardness of your flesh,
Sail across the blue of your own eyes and find the horizon
That is encompassed only by your heart.
Take not these stars as mere playthings
But more,
More beloved,
As guideposts to eternity.

Does it hurt when I do that?

You could at least ask
Does it hurt when you
Twist me and pull me
Bend me and beat me
You could at least ask

You could at least ask
If my tears are real
And my pain complete
In your torments
You could at least ask

You could at least ask
If I needed this
Or desired that
Or deserved to feel
You could at least ask

You could at least ask
When I am shattered
Forgotten and alone
Fearful and frozen
You could at least ask

You could at least ask
If there was any way
That you could lift me
From my sorrows
You could at least ask

You could at least ask
Does it hurt
When I do that?
Does it hurt?
You could at least ask.

I Am

I am the worst part of good
And the best part of evil
I am that ultimate conundrum
That final difficult puzzle
I am a man

Filled with infinite possibilities
I plot the most vile degradations
While still possessing
A tenderness and compassion
That makes angels weep

Simultaneously I can build
Rockets that take me to the stars
And rain death upon my enemies

I can be so enraged
By senseless death and violence
That I will wage war to stop it

I can build hospitals and schools
Playgrounds and missile silos
All with the same tools

I can grasp the infinite
See beyond myself
While still maintaining
Legendary shortsightedness

I am a man

Lilies and Seashells

He seeks lilies in the flower shop and know that none are there
Save for poor remembrances with artificial hues and scent
That takes him not to the sea to the shore to the secret mountain
But instead only to those dusty places that rumble and groan

The truck stop waitress, a ribbon in her hair peers between
Sad curtains stained with rain and food and the countless before
Hates her glancing flickered eyes towards a road she will not take
Waiting for a car she does not want and a driver she would flee

She was a lily once that sat amongst the dappled sun and dreamt
Of he the final gardener who might upon one day discover her
And then replanted taken far to where the salt sea shared a voice
With old sweaters, soft reactions and the songs of seashells

Fiona

Wind tousled hair
And midnight blue eyes
Her face is the moon
Framed with a dark sky
Of oaken curls

Mysteries and questions
A million times deep
Hide behind a perfect brow
And opulent lashes

She dances and twirls
In laughter sparkled air
While songs lap easily
Against me

Her hand in mine
While the wind
Jests playfully
With the hem
Of her skirt
And all is good
In the world

Incantations

Shall we invoke the gods,
Wake them from their ancient slumbers,
Watch as they cast about, shaking hoar frost and the dust of ages
From eyes long sealed?
Shall we call on them to dance,
To join us by fires and the crafts of old women?
Ancient trials and ancient tribulations wash across our bodies,
Hard as stone and creviced with the days.
These are times of magic,
Of muttered words and secret incantations.
Stand with me at water's edge and seek reflections in fire,
Our secrets are there,
Buried amongst the dark sands.
We know these things and more,
And yet we do not share them.
Prometheus tried once
And he pays for it yet.

The gods are jealous in their old age.
They have forgotten love and strength
and the raging of the winds.
We have not.
Our souls are still wet, newborn, unknown.
The blood that drips from them carves channels men sail down,
We hold the heavens aloft and scream at the sun.
New days are coming
Carved to seem like ravens claws
That track upon our porcelain skin.
We will be good, we will be great.
Scatter those ashes into the fire and say the name
we dare not say.
Mutter it forth and frothy at the lips
And see the flames change with dire development,
We will hide naught.

Gran 1918-2004

These crashing waves
Of heart-sore grief
That smash unbidden
Against my façade

You think you're safe
Protected for the moment
Idle time and easy emotion
And then it catches

The jagged nail
The caught breath
The misting eyes
The hollow sore

Toughness is a mask
Easily shattered
By thoughts of you
And thoughts of us

We all hold our sadness
Tightly to ourselves
Unwilling to share
Unable to show

Each a strong show
Of artificial control
And pretend courage
But it's not real

A hole is left
Where once you were
And all we can do
Is sit at the edge and weep

And When The Tears Have Settled

And when the tears have settled
Like ash upon your pale soft cheek
And those final truths darkly hid
Wash against the soul of you
What is left to be said?
That some wounds cut too deep
That all the should haves passed
And what was lost was not a thing
What was thrown away was an us

In Starlight

She spins in starlight
I have seen her
Watched for hours as the sky
Is reflected in her eyes
And there in pools of
Cerulean radiance
Lies secrets and dreams

Lilies

We take turns
In emotional
Mental bondage
Slaves to our desires
Wants needs hopes
Wishes

Desperation and
Silent longing
Our best known
Companions
But I'll walk
With you now

Side by side
Our orbiting
Shadows interlock
And exchange
Positional changes
We can eclipse each other

Hide in each other
Hope in each other
Dream for and with
The other
Just to make the day
That little bit softer

It's Not Always About You

It's not always about you, although once I guess it was
I sought treasure and dug always deeper with dreams
Of sparkling diamonds and fairy tale endings, but no.
No, I found instead just salt that I rubbed so vigorously
Into wounds I'd happily and knowingly cut into me.

It's not always about you, although once I guess it was
I guess it is now, at least now with these last few words
I have no dreams of that anymore, the mask has slipped
And there, there I finally saw that which I had refused
That some things and sometimes the flaws are too deep

It's not always about you, although once I guess it was
But it's not anymore, never will be again, can never be
You sold it cheaply, easily, a dime-store novelty worn once
And then discarded in the haste and emptiness of you
And now I know a saucer of soul could not have fed my heart

It's no longer about you

All Of You

I want to be in you, all of you,
In the deepest recesses,
In all the places where you
Have never been touched,
I want us to scream
With our explorations,
To lay ourselves bare,
To be offerings to each other,
There is no, no. there is no cant,
There is only further,
Turning ourselves inside out
Until we are our own cocoons,
Our own wrappings and rapture.
I am the alien who fell to earth,
The angel discarded,
The human wanting
To be human and missing.
Find me, turn me over, inside out
And tell me what I am
And I will discover you

I am a sore symphony

I am a sore symphony, discordant notes
That flutter amongst leaves where
Once thrummed honest passions.
I placed myself, strings and all,
Burnished wood that glowed
With expectations shining wonder
Into her arms, and there, lay in hope.
For the sake of all the stars I sang,
Annotations in bloods sacred script
Giving all for the notes tremulous,
Bled to ensure the tune was followed
And in the end I was left outside.
A discarded toy rather than a cherished thing

To Retire

   Or, to retire to our chamber
And there feel the warmth
That burns beneath our skin
   To find in passions deepest swoons
A heat that lasts eternally and then,
To blow on gentle embers
And watch them come alight
   Tracing my finger down your chest
I would find the secret opening
To your heart and there,
I will kiss until
The lock releases
And my breath can sneak in
   And in sacred words,
I will speak so that
None can hear
But you can feel
Chants visions
Soft panting moments
Of ecstatic joy and
Memories of things yet to happen
   Oh love, the words you say, the visions you impart

Desperately miss

I so desperately miss
The ideal of you
If not the reality
I ache for the want
Of that personification
Of truth and beauty and love
Even if the nature of it
Was as tenuous as the wind
As solid as a sigh
I miss the thought that
There could be one in whom
Nobility and honour
Were not words written as
A child's empty scribbles
I miss believing in
Something incorruptible
Pure of heart, of mind
I so sadly miss those times
I could see you as
A goddess of unquestioned right
And oh such disservice I did
When all you really wanted
Was to be so much less

Read Not My Palm

Read not my palm for it
Tells only of scars and
Labours hard taskings
Of slips and scrapes and
The sweat of forgotten places
Read not the lines cut deep
Into the once upon a time
Smoothness of my forehead
Read only the tales writ soft
In the dark places of my heart

Fiona Grows

My little girl grows

The ages race before me

Infant and baby

Now there's a child

Would if I could

Stop time

Keep us both

Like this

Forever daddy

Forever baby

But could I deny her

The joys of life

The advantages of age

She deserves

All I've had

And ever so much more

So my tears are hidden

My angst is my own

She wants to grow up

Even if I don't

I will Pray

Gladly I melt within your furnace,
I will be the pyre to warm your hearth,
light the cave from which you view the world.
Prometheus held nothing that burned
so hot, so bright as we do, we shall.
I will be the couch you rest upon,
the canvas for your paint,
Dig deep within me,
take my bones to make brushes.
and when I am spent,
when all of me is in all of you
I will whisper,
I will kneel at the altar of you,
I will pray.

Do not be angry

Do not feel angry with me
For the words I use,
I found them written
On your heart and there
By reading
I took them as my own

Lessons lost

I have no lessons left I told her
As we spoke fondly, emptily
Our words once blazed with
Passions reddest glow but now
We are just fond, waiting
Lying.
All the tears are shed and now
All the words are wasted lost
We fill time to salve the cuts
Made so willfully, maliciously
And now regretted en passant
Losing
I could not have you, take you
Even though I bleed without
The emptiness remains in you
You know but cannot change
Love was never enough so now
Death

I Musica

Lacrimoso
Chambers filled with empty seats and strewn
about, cast away programmes trampled, lost.
Dolce, dolce what lies I made for you to keep,
what dreams and hopes printed, crumpled false
Best had I never awakened from my shrouds
than to have lain amongst the dead and empty
Lacrimoso

Leggiero
These strings, thin sinews that bind in place
I asked only if you touch, you touch gently.
Be kind for I bleed in my hardness, my strength
Keep words and faith and when the curtain falls
as all must , let us find grace in sputtering lime
Let shadows descend as soft as ravens claws
Leggiero

Morendo

Tattered remnants of red, mahogany, even moths
have left the curtains ruin and the stage rotted.
Allegro appasionato, I believed in the notes and keys
followed the harmony I scratched into my flesh and,
waiting but never seeing the composers secret.
The pages were always waiting for the dust to settle.
Morendo

Lacrimoso - Play sadly

Leggiero - Play gently

Morendo - Play to death

Rest

I rest my head upon your lap and
Speak in whispered holy tones
To the small mound of your belly
Look up at you with glowing eyes
Cover my mouth so you cannot hear the secrets
I tell only to your flesh and what lies within.
"Baby," I whisper...
You must know these things, secret and arcane
For once you see the light you must learn more
A tiny phrase of massive proportions,
you, beloved child, hear me and know,
I am your father, lover to your mother,
Servant to you both

Feet

When I kiss your feet,
When they are upon me,
It is not just for
The taste of toes
Or to see the smile
Upon your face.
It is not to love
Their gentle elegance,
Their shape,
It is for another reason.
It is so I can be
For one brief
And glorious moment,
The very earth you walk upon

Lost

You said once
That if I was lost
You would come
And find me
Never did I expect
That you
Would be the one
To lose me

Sphere

I would catch the moon for her

Tame the silvery sphere

To hang from her wrist

The stars would kneel

And be woven amongst

Her wild hanging curls

The sun would set only

To rest upon her finger

And the eternal firmament

Would caress her shoulders

A shawl to stop the chill

And even with these things

She would still outshine

Them all

Dream of Wet

Obsidian roads hiss under

A starless sky

A serpent stretched from

There to nowhere, to you

To a dawn that threatens

To memories false and

Cherished like a newborn

This darkness this rain this hour

Brought forth for

Amusement, rash sorrow

The air smells of the sea

A deep green of recollection

Of places never seen and

Best of all of dreams never caught

Run from me, faster still

Stay always at horizons edge

Let me strive and ache

And there in my place

Draw the earth about me

Let me dream of wet

Many Miles

Many miles wandered lost
To find that brow and there upon
Leave such kisses and devotions
For all that is so good and noble

Sea and land do so deceive
Where weary bones and souls depart
And yet I struggle o'er them all
For she that is deserving such

Oh cruel fates for now I've learned
The error of my simple ways
That distance great is on no map
But 'tween a maidens heart and truth

Prisoners

Prisoners of love
We kneel in cages
Hoping only that
Our jailers will not
Be too cruel
For hearts are
Too easily broken
By the lightest
And most savage
Of touches

Canvases

We are sore canvases
Lines crudely drawn
An excess of reds of
Deep tissue purples and
The magenta of all
Our gathered sorrows
When we should seek
The softest hues of
Painted memory all
Tinted with an artist's
Loving touch

Nestled

And nestled here within my arms,
This poor frame a sad imperfect mattress for your limbs,
I can speak only in whispered tones,
Delicate resolutions, hushed intonations.
Hush child I say, hear the silences I impart and know
That all is safe and all is quiet in these hours.
I offer no glimpses of perfection nor heavenly resolution
But only these joints too hard and muscles too soft.
Of all the things that have left me bereft,
Of all my scars and broken down parts
None have touched my soul, my love, my dreams.
Those I kept safe away till now,
Till here, till I press them gently against your heart and say
Hush, child, you are safe here, nestled within my arms.

The Truth of Love

The truth of love
The truth of us
The truth of lies
And worse
The truth of lies believed
Sworn promise on
Bended knee and
Heart flayed wide
To say
I will not love this way again

Morning

Soft brown tangles

Luxurious curls

Muttered incoherencies

Through half asleep dreams

She smiles in the gloom

And her hands

Go about my neck

Good morning daddy

And into my arms

Nestled tight

For the start

Of a new day

Hair

Long luxurious hair,
Spread like
The peacocks fan
Across a pillow.

Dreams of Bacchus
And Saturnalian delights.

To shorn it
Is to cut away
Mystery and allure.

Let that hair enrobe me,
Let it caress my chest
Like downy feathers,

Let it curl
And coil across me,
Bathing me in silk
And perfumes rich.

Wave it like a mane
And give the wind
A new plaything
So that
I may become jealous
At its unbridled
Caresses.

Apollo

Apollo mocks with cruelties deep
To see me brought asunder
To laugh and howl while I do weep
And watch the temples plunder

Oh gods Olympians I beg of thee
To tell me of my follies made
From where my tears and death of glee
Force me from my peaceful glade

Oh Eros come and stop thy weeping
Your crimes are known for all to see
It is for love our angers keeping
We live to see such tragedy

For you did love with all your heart
A mortal woman made of clay
And now your temples torn apart
You join the gods this very day

And Eros from his knees did rise
To see Apollo weeping
To see true love that rots and dies
And virtues not for keeping

And she with silver hair

And she with silver hair, with memory etched in skin
She remembered him once and thought him long gone

What had been his end of days, so long ago so far away
Did he remember me when the dusk came or was I a ghost
I had forgotten him till now, this man, this shade from my past
His name had all but slipped from memory and love
Too many days that curled yellow into years and were lost
Too many new voices that drowned the memory of him
And did he think kindly of me ever again, did he smile
Or was all that happened and all that was not etched too deep
Did he still regret those not born, those that never were
Did he sigh for orange rooms lost in dust and filled with ashes

She wondered if he forgot as well, if she had slipped from him
But she knew in her heart, in the empty place she had left him
That he had not, that he would not, that 'till his eyes grew dim
He would remember it all with the clarity of a hurt child
And she, now with silver hair, now with old bones and memory
Had been the one who drew the blade and made the red to fall

Your Arms

Your arms about me, hold me tight,
Press me to your flesh and then,
Thrust in the blade, sink it deep
As I sink into you, pin us together,
Carve runes in my heart,
Drink the wine of my veins
And we shall howl until the gods flee in fear.
We will be the ancient offerings,
The new salvation.
You found me first,
Dug me out of the ground and
Pried the coins from my eyes.
Awakened not with a kiss but
With riding heat and nails
That gouge my flesh and bring utterances,
Mewls, moans. There is no pity here,
Only hunger

Gabriel

   Gabriel presses his fingertip
Above a babies lips
To tell them to be silent
About the glories
Of heaven
   Gabriel presses his fingertip
Above my heart
To tell me to stop weeping
A love that's lost
Was never mine
   I smile and ask
Beloved angel, friend
Will there ever be
A day not sorrowed
Or is it my lot
To lose my heart
   Faith my son, have faith
For you alone
Must carry the truth
That love is lost
By those that are as well
Now rest

I Lied

I lied to her every day
I told her those things
The great falsehoods
Of life, my life, all life
I lied to her every day
I said that love mattered
I said that love conquered
I said that faith and hope
Charity and kindness
Would always win
I lied to her every day

She never believed my lies

Craig Murray
You Spoke Volumes

You spoke volumes

In your silence

Turned your head away

When I said I love you

Pretending not to hear

Words you once said

In earnest, in whispers

You spoke volumes

In your silence

Sighing in annoyance

At my asking if you knew

I still remembered

All we might have been

All we never were

You spoke volumes

In your silence

Until all I could do

Was match you

Wordlessly silently

And now forever

You spoke volumes

In your silence

A Voice

I found a voice in her,

Wrapped amongst the hems of her skirt,

It was a thing I had forgotten,

Hoarse I was,

Dry as the desert,

Lost.

I found a voice in her

That sang a song of praise

Of ancient and wanted things,

Of memory,

Of love.

Sand had choked the passage

And the rooms were empty

Save for old cups,

Tears,

Lost things of distances.

When her wind blew,

When the trees danced,

When old men raised their eyes skyward

And smiled at the gods,

She was here.

I found a voice in her

Would you miss me?

Would you miss me
Were I gone,
Would the air still
Or the skies darken.
Would you sigh wistfully
And move on,
A leaf that falls in a stream,
The passing flock.
Would you wonder
One day
What had become of me.

Would you miss me
Were I gone,
Would you search for me,
Pine for me,
Ache for me.
Would fingers scrabble
At hard earth,
Stones,
Would knees be scraped
And elbows bleed in your search.
Would I be
An eternal search
Or a passing wisp
That blew through your hair?

Pablos inheritor

She quoted Pablo with a voice matured and seasoned with artifice and want.
Looking deep into his eyes she smiled sweetly and crooned,

'I do not love you as if you were salt-rose, or topaz,'

She recited his words as if they were her own, not copied from a book.
Pablo's soul was reconstituted into a whisper sent to a desperate heart and needful ears.
He sat enraptured across from her and ached as he felt his love grow with her words,
His heart soar in her hand, his soul healed of carried terrors.
What she should just have said is, "I do not love you."

Lilacs

We sat, she and I beneath
The lilacs fragrant gaiety.
Long, warm, languid hours
Of ease, eternal quiet.
Our brows unfurrowed by
Mankind's trivialities.
The language of crinoline,
Stroked hair and gazes.
There is nothing more needed
Nothing desired or wanted.
Just soft ease and those
Rare gentle times of noon.
And with the setting of the sun
We might slip into shadows.

Tattooed by your words

The ache to possess a thing
As simple as a word
As complex as a thought
As beautiful as a dream.
To read them once and sigh
Knowing that it's not enough
Will never be enough
And so I tattoo myself
With your words
Pasted wet to my skin
I can read them in the soft places
The hard places
The curves and joints of me
Where they settle and I hope
Sigh a bit for me

Will you stay my little girl forever?

Will you stay my little girl forever?
I beg of you,
Remain here, in my arms,
Your head on my chest,
Your tiny face smiling up at mine.
You have given me a soul
I never had before,
A life,
I never knew.

When I hold you
I hold the universe in my hands
I hold immortality
But all I want
Is for you to always be my sweetheart
My little girl

You lie your head upon my chest
And your eyes flutter
With the exhaustion of your day
A deep breath
A settling
And my heart melts
That little sigh you make
That personal hush
That descends and envelops you
Until you awake with a smile
Or a laugh
Or even to pull my beard.

Watching Her Walk

Your many facets
Your features
The wise man, the fool,
The angel and the devil
All take a seat upon your brow
And leave their mark while
The moment takes you
I love them all

We talk at length
Neither of us making sense
Noises and laughter,
An infant's best language
They sparkle as they
Splash around the room
They lighten your soul
Where they touch
They make the day brighter

I saw a calendar today
And looked up all your birthdays
I almost wept.
Let's both of us stay this way
Let's both of us
Remain, here in this room
You
My baby girl
Me
The devoted faultless father

Time may give me
Faults in your eyes
But now
I just evoke smiles.

Will you stay my little girl forever?

Stay With Me A Little While

Stay with me a little while, as the lights dim,

As my fingers grow colder and the sun in my soul sets.

Sit here, abide with me,

There are no harsh words now,

The door is barred,

The windows shuttered and this house,

This place grows silent.

I have put away those final things,

Stacked the papers and the books

Where they can be gathered or discarded.

Lie back, let us speak of ghosts and memory,

Of all things that have passed like water

Beneath the hull of us.

And Who Am I?

And who am I she asked
Mere curiosity, passing wonder
You, you who were once
The very folds of my heart
Whose name meant truth
And in whose eyes I prayed
Supplicant before the temple
You were the very water
For the desert that I was
The reason I believed again
My hope for all that might be
Ancient runes I carved in flesh
To spell your secret name and
By whispering it evoke magic
Who are you, who did you become
Or always were in waiting
Just some girl, just some lie
I told myself to keep the dark away

And when she was spoken of

And when she was spoken of
It was in words drawn from
The edges of my heart, my soul
They were the words I knew
Without speaking, without saying
She was my sun and my moon
She was my brilliant dawn
She was my sultry night of stars
She held truth in her eyes
She was my word for love
She was hope and want and lust

And when I spoke of her
These are the things I said
Unfailingly, unhesitatingly
She was "Oh love"
She was the mother of the twins
She was all I dreamed her of being
And then, when I was dust
When I was discarded and forgotten
And all those asked who came
After me
What was she to them
They replied quickly
She was easy, I fucked her

Black Stains

You need to write this on your arms
Permanent markers black stains
Or better yet
Carve it in your flesh, bleed memory
Down the left you may engrave
He never gave up on us, we meant something
And then on the right, carve deeply
He never gave up on me, even though I did
And when the room grows dim
When all is said and nothing remains
As my limbs chill and I wait
I will watch to see the door open and
You come in
I never gave up easily because
I refuse for both of us to fail

Come

Come to me my love and lay
Your head upon my chest
And dream that we rest
In sacred luxury of lovers
Where all the world sighs
To gaze upon the perfection
Of two souls thus entwined
And two hearts thus enjoyed

She Cries

But I love you she writes
A plaintive cry that
Cuts my heart and leaves
All the parts of me awash
In all that was and worse
All that should have been
And oh how I ache for her
For that gentle touch and
The gentle words that left
All of me in comforted ease
When life was answered in
Softest voice that whispered
All will be right in the world
As long as you remember
Love

Found Poems

I found poems in her hair
In the way she touched my cheek
Scattered lilies diamonds and
The gold veneer of love that wraps
My beating heart
Come to me my love and rest
Within these hollow arms
That have no purpose without you

Words

Words bear magic, meaning, suitcases of dreams, hopes,
Pack-sacks wrapped in silver, bound in threads drawn
From hearts and eyes and in our whispered dreams

And when found hollow, where ancient timbers rot and
The looseness of the earth gathers in mossy decrepitude
We are lost, adrift amongst the tatters, hollow sockets

Grey sky times, dread loss of all that was, what smallness,
These dreams now seemed to be

I Have no poems

I have no poems left for you
I checked that jar so marked
"That which never was" and there
Amongst the dust and shadows
I sadly saw it now was empty

These words hard formed
Where once a glance would do
To cause the visions to tumble
And words alight upon my soul
As petals from a sated heart.

And oh to go from meaningful
To meaningless and now bereft
To see not sun or silvered moon
That once so illuminated my all
Replaced by empty disregard

You may yet see in years to come
Such mutterings as pen to ink I try
But know you must that echoes sound
And mirrors do reflect, but in that place
My songs and psalms are for another

We never did decide that date when
Love in fleeting splendour bloomed
And waking up still in a kiss did matter
But know we always valentine the day
When love was truly lost for evermore

So hard this was for me to write
So strange to have my muse so fled
That she to whom I pledged my all
evokes no passions, plays or songs
I have no poems left for you

Exeunt

I will remember thee.

I will remember thee.
Solid hours
And dark distress.
I will remember
Thy grasp,
Cold and hungry,
Seeking me out
For vengeful gnawing
On tired bones.
I will remember,
Even though
The days are past,
For smiles may fade
But tears remain
Forever.

Nightsong

Gowned and bejeweled
In the gossamer robes
Of artifice and stars
She spins and dances
In soft moonlight
Hair a thousand hues
Teases faint melodies
As it kisses the fruit
Of her neck
I long to dance with her
My dark mistress
Enraptures and imprisoned
In her eternal embrace
And if she will have me
The song will continue
And forever's steps
Will echo in my mind

Where Poets Die

I found a place where
Poets come to die
Words once loved
Lie scattered like ash
And all the oranges
Soft hues vivid love
Turn grey and fade
With each lie told
And as I nestle in
Amongst the corpses
Broken pens and
Tear stained pages
I still pray for the dawn
Even though it never
Shone upon me

In the Mist

I looked for you there
Within the mist
Within the rosy cheeks
Within the lovers who laughed
At frozen diamonds that clung
To eyelashes, lips, dreams
I looked for you there beside
The great torrents cascade
But you were not there,
Only ice remained

Evermore

Dewdrop comforters that wrap about
The slender wonder of your heart
And hold within such uttered secrets
That paint the mountain ochre rust

I kneel before in resolutions chains
To feel and find that lone horizon
Counted blessings and the hyacinth
Placed upon my chest as warning

Remain I shall for speeding Dawn
Approaches with its noisome thunder
But we alone did cast about in dark
And with that girl who chanted

Evermore

Rough

These slates that build beneath my skin
Rough cut and there in secret written
Words I cast on endless shores forgot
Pale glory is thy name and risen fierce
You climb aboard to take the sea of me
And for our trouble slumbers lost again
Well tethered by word and deed I rise
And fall in crumbling ash and waters
To swirl and there beneath the tide
I sleep

Not Far From Here

There is a place
Not far from here
Where dawn breaks
Eternally
Where children's laughter
And butterflies
Share the sky with
Soft wings

There is a place
Not far from here
Where sun drenched
Kisses
And marble ladies
Shine forever
Under a deep blue
Heaven

There is a place
Not far from here
Where all is soft
And easy
On cool grass and
Shady hills

There is a place
Not far from here
Where fathers hold
Daughters
Forever safe
Comforted in
Strong arms

There is a place
Not far from here
Where we will love
And laugh
Play and run
For all our days

Glorious Dawn

You are my glorious dawn, my sultry moon
Desiccated I lie beneath the broad petals
Of your flower and there I wait for chance.
A drop of your love rolled easily to drip
And bring my salty sands to fruitfulness
The desert harshness fades as colours
Radiance unmatched fill my horizon
The hues of you, the multiplicity of love
There is magic in your breath whispered
It caresses over me and my heart beats
Roaring torrents fill my veins and then
I breathe a first breath of eternities joy
The sand rolls away forgotten jewels
And rising I kneel at petals scented edge
To dip my face into the fragrance of you

The Arroyo Sighs For Lack Of Water

The arroyo sighs for lack of water
Sand keeps memory of rain
While the plants dream of wet
I am that place, that thing
I have bathed in the running cool
I felt the splash of life
(She washed the sins from the palms of my hands
with her kisses)
And when the rains ended
When life soaked into the sky
And the white boiled blue away
I lay steaming upon the ground
Hoping the clouds
Will not forget me
(Remember the way that she slept with me
and kept me safe)

She in The Garden

And she knelt there in the dark, the silence
Knees covered in loose dirt, leaves, memory
So you know this man who weaves words
And leaves you pleading your case amongst
We who will listen, smile at your protestations?

I do she said, head bowed, eyes glistening
He spoke to me of truth and love, dignity
In glowing words he laid himself before me
And offered me horizons than shone eternal
He asked only of love for love and kindness
Such simple things, so little and yet they weighed
So heavily upon my brow until I wept bitterly
These things he asked me for, for my sake
More ever than for his, to save me from myself

Craig Murray *Watching Her Walk*

And did you listen, child, lost in these woods?
His advice and love, his hope for you, for all
Those things he asked for, so little, so little
And yet you are here, kneeling amongst olives
Soiled knees and back bent, a stain upon you
Willingly and intentionally you called centurion
Brought us from our rounds, brought us to you
and rutting beasts do hold themselves less cheap
but still child, you brought us here knowing
how small a price he asked you pay for love
that dignity and truth once lost are forever gone
while stains on the chin might be wiped away
the stains on your soul are yours eternally
so all that I ask is this, you of hollow want
you sell yourself cheaply, you do the same to him
what reason could you have to come here with us

I will do what is right for me she says waiting
While another aligns with her dripping worth
So before you take him, take me but first oh first
Pay me my wages while you plow, thirty silver.

Love

And oh I love fiercely, keep your temerity
I want to love so it hurts, so it boils
I want to feel it in every part of me, ache from it
Need it, live it, breathe in great gasping breaths
As I surface from it, only to sink beneath again
I want love to mean, to count, to need and
I want love to love.
Keep your entertainments, your flirtings
Keep your playthings as hollow and empty as
The souls of the self desecrated, abandoned,
I want nothing to do with them, leave them
Those temporary lovers, passing fancies
They may whittle away the hours but only
The hours till you die
No, never, I will not be sold cheaply and
I will never love falsely, let me rage in my love
Let me boil over with it and then oh glorious
Let it burn within until I am but ash upon it
My heart though scarred beats louder still
I rise within my love and know my love and there
Only there is my truth

I love

www.ingramcontent.com/pod-product-compliance
Lightning Source LLC
LaVergne TN
LVHW041625070426
835507LV00008B/448